Martin Luther King, Jr. Day

by Meredith Dash

ABDO
NATIONAL HOLIDAYS
Kids

www.abdopublishing.com

Published by Abdo Kids, a division of ABDO, PO Box 398166, Minneapolis, Minnesota 55439.

Printed in the United States of America, North Mankato, Minnesota.

052014

092014

 **THIS BOOK CONTAINS RECYCLED MATERIALS**

Photo Credits: AP Images, Corbis, Getty Images, Shutterstock, © ags1973 even pages,
© spirit of america p.9, © Steve Heap p.19, © EPG_EuroPhotoGraphics p.21 / Shutterstock.com

Production Contributors: Teddy Borth, Jennie Forsberg, Grace Hansen

Design Contributors: Candice Keimig, Laura Rask, Dorothy Toth

Library of Congress Control Number: 2013952320

Cataloging-in-Publication Data

Dash, Meredith.

 Martin Luther King, Jr. Day / Meredith Dash.

  p. cm. -- (National holidays)

ISBN 978-1-62970-045-8 (lib. bdg.)

Includes bibliographical references and index.

1. Martin Luther King, Jr., Day--Juvenile literature. 2. King, Martin Luther, Jr., 1929-1968--Juvenile
literature. I. Title.

323--dc23

2013952320

Table of Contents

Martin Luther King, Jr. 4

Martin Luther King, Jr. Day. 8

When We Celebrate 18

How We Celebrate. 20

More Facts 22

Glossary 23

Index 24

Abdo Kids Code. 24

Martin Luther King, Jr.

Martin Luther King, Jr. was a great **civil rights** leader.

4

5

King was shot and killed on April 4, 1968. The nation was saddened.

ARTIN LUTHER KING JR.
29 — 1968
AST, FREE AT LAST,
MIGHTY I'M FREE AT LAST."

7

Martin Luther King, Jr. Day

On June 26, The King Center was **founded**. It celebrated the first MLK, Jr. Day.

8

9

In 1973, Illinois signed

MLK, Jr. Day into law.

But people wanted it

to be a **national holiday**.

PROTEST NOW AGAINST:
HIGHWAY PATROL FOR
BLACKS

PROTEST NOW AGAINST
COLUMBIA POLICE DEPT.
BRUTALITY-AGAINST
SLED ...VER UP

PROTE... NOW AGAINST
...DERS &
...UP

11

Mrs. King spoke before **Congress**. She wanted MLK, Jr. Day to be a **national holiday**. But most were against it.

13

Senator Ted Kennedy promised to help. On October 19, 1983, the **bill** passed.

15

On November 3, 1983,

MLK, Jr. Day became a

national holiday. President

Ronald Reagan signed it into law.

16

17

When We Celebrate

We celebrate MLK, Jr. Day

every third Monday in January.

INJUSTICE ANYWHERE IS A THREAT TO JUSTICE EVERYWHERE. WE ARE
CAUGHT IN AN INESCAPABLE NETWORK OF MUTUALITY, TIED IN
A SINGLE GARMENT OF DESTINY. WHATEVER AFFECTS
ONE DIRECTLY AFFECTS ALL INDIRECTLY.

19

How We Celebrate

On this day, we honor Martin Luther King, Jr. We remember his good works. We celebrate community and **equality**.

THE ANNUAL
MARTIN LUTHER KING, JR.
HOLIDAY MEMORIAL MARCH

21

More Facts

- Martin Luther King, Jr. was arrested nearly 30 times while supporting the **Civil Rights Movement**.

- Martin Luther King, Jr.'s most famous speech is his "I Have a Dream" speech. He delivered it in front of over 200,000 people on August 28, 1963, on the steps of the Lincoln Memorial in Washington, D.C.

- At age 35, King was the youngest person to receive the **Nobel Peace Prize**.

Glossary

bill – a proposal for a new law.

Civil Rights Movement – the public fight for civil rights for all citizens. Civil rights include the right to vote and freedom of speech.

Congress – a lawmaking body in the United States. It is made up of the Senate and the House of Representatives. It meets in Washington, D.C. to reject or accept bills.

equality – everyone being treated the same.

found – establish or create.

national holiday – also known as a federal holiday, a special event celebrated by a country.

Nobel Peace Prize – an award given for doing something to help make peace in the world.

Index

civil rights 4

Congress 12

Illinois 10

King Center, The 8

Martin Luther King
4, 6, 20, 22

Mrs. King 12

national holiday 10, 12, 16

Ronald Reagan 16

Ted Kennedy 14

abdokids.com

Use this code to log on to abdokids.com and access crafts, games, videos and more!

Abdo Kids Code:
NMK0458